1800 WOODCUTS
BY THOMAS BEWICK
AND HIS SCHOOL

Edited by Blanche Cirker
and the Editorial Staff of Dover Publications

With an Introduction by
Robert Hutchinson

Dover Publications, Inc., New York

Published in Canada by General Publishing Company, Ltd.,
30 Lesmill Road, Don Mills, Toronto, Ontario.

Published in the United Kingdom by Constable and Company, Ltd.,
10 Orange Street, London WC 2.

1800 Woodcuts by Thomas Bewick and His School is a new selection of illustrations by Thomas Bewick and his collaborators and imitators, and is first published in 1962.

This volume also contains a new Introduction written especially for this edition by Robert Hutchinson.

1800 Woodcuts by Thomas Bewick and His School belongs to the Dover Pictorial Archive Series. Up to ten illustrations from this book may be reproduced on any one project or in any single publication, free, and without special permission. Wherever possible include a credit line indicating the title of this book, author, and publisher. Please address the publisher for permission to make more extensive use of illustrations in this book than that authorized above.

The republication of this book in whole is prohibited.

International Standard Book Number: 0-486-20766-8
Library of Congress Catalog Card Number: 62-51830

Manufactured in the United States of America

DOVER PUBLICATIONS, INC.
180 Varick Street
New York, N. Y. 10014

INTRODUCTION

Thomas Bewick, England's foremost wood engraver, was born in August, 1753, at Cherryburn House, near Eltringham in Northumberland, where his father owned a farm and small coal mine. The eldest of eight children, the boy enjoyed a lively childhood devoted less to books and learning than to pranks, rambles along the river Tyne, and chores on his father's farm. From an early age he showed signs of artistic talent, and although he had seen no paintings other than the king's arms in church and the boards of the four local taverns, he soon began covering the margins of his exercise books, the stones of the church porch, and the family hearth with drawings of battles, wild beasts, and birds. At fourteen he was apprenticed to a Newcastle engraver whose business was the etching of ornamental silver and billheads; because the owner, Ralph Beilby, was unable to execute occasional requests from printers for wood engravings, the work fell to his apprentice, who soon became so adept at the unfamiliar technique that one of his blocks, "The Huntsman and the Old Hound," won him a seven-guinea award from the Society for the Encouragement of the Arts. Released from his apprenticeship, Bewick sought work in

London but found the city crowded, dirty, and unfriendly. Returning to his beloved Northumberland, he opened a shop at Newcastle with his brother John, and for the next fifty years produced, with his pupils and associates, a series of woodblocks so skillful that for the first time wood engraving became an art in England. In 1785 Bewick began work on the cuts for the book that was to make him famous — his *General History of Quadrupeds* — and in 1797 and 1804 published the two volumes of his greatest work, his *History of British Birds*. For the next twenty years he produced few books of importance, but labored diligently in his shop, where Audubon found him "a perfect old Englishman" who worked in a soiled nightcap and slept at night wrapped in a blanket on the floor. Bewick died November 8, 1828, at the age of 75, and is buried at Ovingham churchyard, across the river from Cherryburn House where he was born.

Bewick was the complete artist, who never tired of refining his techniques and who designed tailpieces ("talepieces" as he called them) for diversion in his leisure hours after his day's work of engraving billheads and bottle molds. Again and again he rearranged into new forms the materials of his Tyneside childhood — the sight of a kite caught on a man's hat, of boys riding on gravestones, vermin-hunting expeditions in the snow, lambs sheltered from the cold. His accomplishment, however, was much more than that of the genre artist. He brought to perfection an art form hardly in existence at the time of his birth, and in doing so radically altered methods of book production and illustration for the next hundred years.

Before Bewick's time the woodcut was known primarily as practiced by its German masters, who carved with a knife on the plank side of the wood and achieved a bold and somewhat austere effect. Long in decline, it was seldom used for quantity book production; when eighteenth-century publishers wished illustrations, they turned rather to copper engravings, the elegance of which seemed more in keeping with the neo-classical spirit of the age. Bewick, attracted to the homelier qualities of wood, worked with the graver on the end rather than the plank side of the wood, and was able to provide both the durability (some blocks withstanding as many as 900,000 impressions) and meticulous detail necessary for book work. By lowering the block and varying the width of his strokes, he could obtain remarkable effects of distance and tone. The result was a form of artwork completely in harmony with the crisp clarity of type. From Bewick's death until the introduction of photo-engraving in 1880, wood engraving was the primary means of book and periodical illustration in England and abroad.

If Bewick's method was new, so was his subject matter. He came at a time when men of sensibility were first beginning to see nature as if it were brand-new, and in turning his back on London for simple Northumberland scenes (as in rejecting copper engravings for the plainer effects of wood) Bewick was foreshadowing the Romantic Revival and working in the spirit of James Thomson, Burns, and later, John Clare. It is not without significance that Charlotte Brontë at sixteen wrote a poem about Bewick, or that the book Jane Eyre found so mysteriously exciting at the beginning of her romantic story was Bewick's *History of British Birds*. "O that the genius of Bewick were mine," wrote Wordsworth in *Lyrical Ballads*, and Carlyle and Ruskin echoed the praise.

In Bewick's case the return to nature was simple and unforced: he could hardly do otherwise. The country of his childhood filled his imagination, seeming, according to his *Memoir*, "altogether a paradise to me." He loved its people, their superstitions and robust amusements, and looked with affection upon its smallest detail: the symmetry of a woodcock's feather, bird's eggs silent in the grass. As one familiar with the problems of crossing country streams, he depicts a dozen ways of doing it — of crossing on stilts, seizing the low-hanging branch that leaves the dog behind, the difficult crossing of the blind, or, most touchingly, that of the man who carries his entire family — wife and child — on his back on his way across. If there is wit in these small prints, there is often an almost heartbreaking tenderness too, for all that he depicts is traced with great care and great love.

It is, indeed, Bewick's warmth and tenderness that endear him to us today and explain the singular charm and intimacy his work will always have. His work is, in the deepest sense of the term, completely personal. His last tailpiece, for example — completed shortly before his death — shows a funeral procession winding down the hill from Cherryburn House, Bewick's birthplace, to the ferry that will cross the river Tyne to Bewick's grave in Ovingham churchyard. Few artists have revealed their inner life in their work more intimately or more unobtrusively.

Yet Bewick is never without a subject. It is the world of concrete objects that fascinates him, and there seems to be no end to what he attempts on wood, from frogs in conversation to a catalogue of street criers. Even the most complicated genre illustration seems to offer no problems: he shows us the child about to pull the nervous colt's tail, the mother running in terror, and the scene becomes easily understandable, clear, and forever fixed—all in little more than an inch of engraving. Asked how Bewick could create with such skill when he had had no instruction, members of his family replied, almost with wonder, "He used to go out and look at things, and then come home and draw them."

It is when he wanders outside his familiar world that his work suffers. His city scenes and costumes seem stiff and unreal, and even his *Quadrupeds*, many of them copied from museum reconstructions and Buffon's *Natural History*, appear less vivid than his *Birds*, which he drew from life (the swallow running so close to the graver that it almost interfered with his work) or from models brought to him by sporting friends. Here Bewick is at his best. The birds seem ready to fly from the page, and of each he presents the very essence, from the self-important pose of the starling to the face of the small owl that seems to be permanently surprised. The wrens, robins, blackbirds, and crows he had seen outside his window as a child at Cherryburn House had now come alive in his work, and even the Chillingham bull, considered by Bewick his best work and sketched at great personal danger to himself, fades in comparison.

Bewick trained many pupils in his Newcastle shop — such workers as Charlton Nesbit, Luke Clennell, William Harvey, Henry Hole, William Temple, and John Jackson — and it was they, rather than members of his own family, who were to carry on his work during his declining years. His son, Robert Elliot Bewick, was in poor health all his life, and Bewick's brother, John Bewick, who showed signs of a promising talent, died in 1795 at the age of 35. The pupils, however — notably Nesbit,

Clennell, and Harvey — managed to produce a large amount of work in the Bewick vein before wood engraving fell to Branston, Landells, Whymper, and Sears in the period of its greatest flourishing after Bewick's death.

It is the very similarity of much of this work that has created the difficult problems of identification with which collectors of Bewick are familiar. Many of Bewick's pupils consciously imitated him; an additional difficulty was the cooperative nature of Bewick's shop, whereby one man might design a block and another execute it, or one man finish cutting what another had begun. In this respect Bewick's shop was typical of its period: the important thing was the work itself rather than the identity of its creator. As a result, however, much that has been claimed as genuine Bewick material is undoubtedly the work of other hands. Of the many books, for example, claimed as Bewick's, probably only the *Quadrupeds* and the two volumes of *Birds* (with some question even about the second volume) were designed and executed exclusively by Bewick himself.

Obviously such identification must be left to the art researcher or scholar and cannot be entered into by this book, which makes no claim to being a work of Bewick scholarship. The limitations of publishing have made that undertaking impossible, rewarding and significant as it might be; and it is rather to the reader that the task must fall of deciding what is Bewick's and not Bewick's in these pages. The editors of Dover Publications, Inc., have, they feel, fulfilled their obligation in that direction by providing an Appendix giving the source of each illustration, keyed to a complete bibliography of works used.

The purpose of this book is rather to make available, in much the way that Bewick and his school did, a rich repository of illustrative material that will prove useful to contemporary artists, designers, illustrators and others in their work. The volume is therefore, we hope, in the spirit of Bewick, and it tries to present, not the definitive Bewick, but the predominant Bewick image.

More than most artists, Bewick established the pictorial symbolism of his age, the clichés, if you will, in which we still tend to think of eighteenth-century England — the small house in the snow, the lamb with its mother, the cat seated in the window. No other artist had to add to this imagery because it was already complete when Bewick passed it on, so that even Alexander Anderson, the father of American wood engraving, frankly imitated it after seeing examples of Bewick's work in 1794. We recognize and resort to this symbolism today. Our purposes may be less serious, but we pay token to Bewick by borrowing the pictorial metaphor in which he cloaked his age.

It is this image — work characteristic of Bewick — that the editors of Dover Publications have sought to present in this volume. We have eliminated such work of Bewick's own as differed from it, and we have included as well work which is obviously not Bewick's but part of the Bewick tradition. In this way we have hoped best to represent Bewick's contribution to art and, at the same time, offer his work in the spirit in which it was produced — for specific use. Artist that he was, Bewick yet created many stock cuts which could be used in a variety of practical ways. It is to be hoped that modern methods of photographic reproduction, far from diminishing the usefulness of engravings such as these, will give them a new lease on life. If so, this book of Thomas Bewick and his school will have fulfilled its purpose.

Robert Hutchinson

New York, New York
July, 1961

CONTENTS

BUSINESS AND TRADES

NATURAL HISTORY

1   The Irish Greyhound

2   The Old English Hound

3   The Newfoundland Dog

4   The Mastiff

6   The Dalmatian or Coach Dog

5   The Harrier

7   The Springer or Cocker

PLATE 1

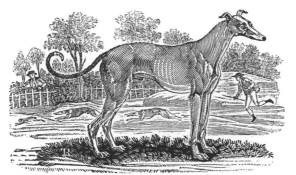

1   The Greyhound

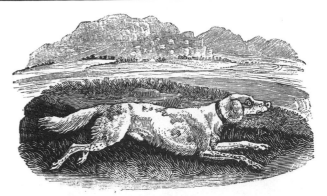

2   The English Setter

3   The Small Water-Spaniel

4   The Large Water-Spaniel

5   The Shepherd's Dog

6   The Bull-Dog

7

8   The Terrier

9   The Comforter

10   The Turnspit

PLATE 2

1   The Lurcher

2   The Beagle

3   The Spanish Pointer

4   The Cur Dog

5   The Ban-Dog

6   The Greenland Dog

7   The Fox Hound

8   The Large Rough Water Dog

PLATE 3

1

2

3

4

5

6

7

8

9

10

11

12

13

PLATE 4

1

2

3

4

5

6

7

8

9

10

PLATE 5

1

2   The Hunter

3   The Improved Cart-Horse

4   The Black Horse

5   The Arabian Horse

6   The Old English Road-Horse

7   The Common Cart-Horse

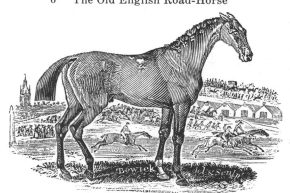

8   The Race Horse

PLATE 6

1

2

3

4

5

6

7

8

PLATE 7

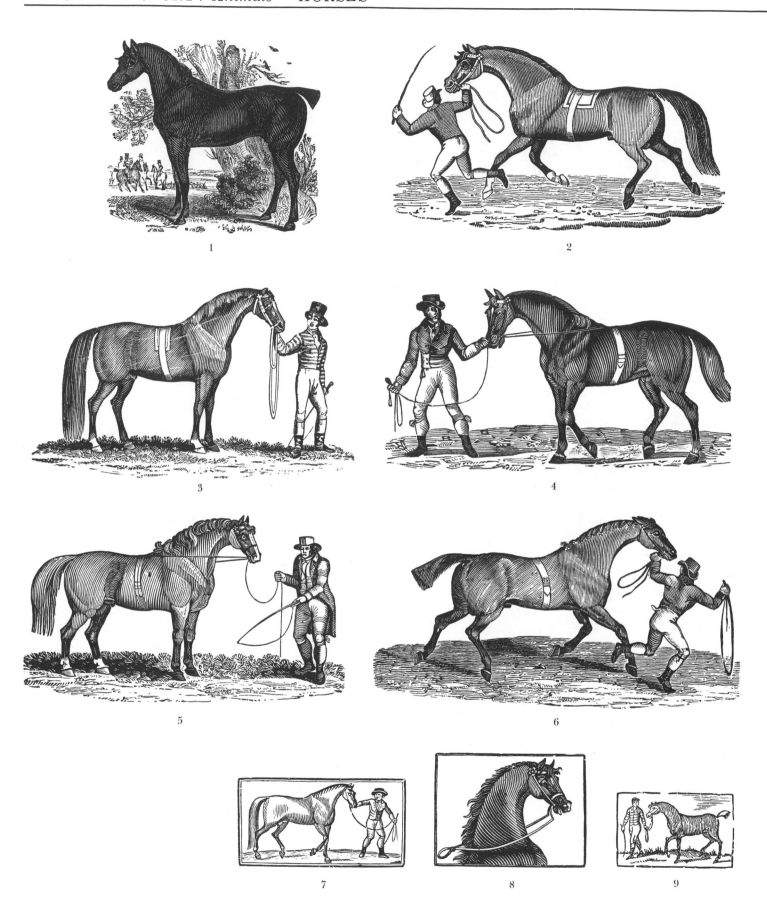

1

2

3

4

5

6

7

8

9

PLATE 8

1   The Mule

2   The Ass

3

4

5

6

PLATE 9

1   The Arabian Camel

2   The Bactrian Camel

3   The Cameleopard

4   The Zebra

PLATE 10

1

PLATE 11

1   The Long-Horned or Lancaster Breed

2   The Improved Holstein or Dutch Breed

3   The Holstein or Dutch Breed

4   Wild Cattle

5   Wild Cattle

6   The Improved Holstein or Dutch Breed

7   The Lancashire Ox

8   The Holstein or Dutch Breed

PLATE 12

1

2

3

4

5

6

7

8

9

10

11

12

13

PLATE 13

1   The Buffalo

2   The Zebu

3   The Urus or Wild Bull

4   The Bison

5   The Musk-Bull

PLATE 14

1   Tees-Water Improved Breed

2   Tees-Water Old or Unimproved Breed

3   The Cheviot Ram

4   The Wedder of Mr. Culley's Breed

5   The Dunky or Dwarf Sheep

6   The Leicestershire Improved Breed

7

PLATE 15

1   The Goat of Angora

2   The Ibex

3   The Mouflon or Musmon

4   The Black-Faced or Heath Ram

5   The Syrian Goat

6   The Common Goat

PLATE 16

1   The Chamois Goat

2   Heath Ram of the Improved Breed

3   The Many-Horned Sheep

4   The Wallachian Sheep

5

6   The Tartarian Sheep

7

8

PLATE 17

1   The Sow of the Improved Breed

2   The Peccary or Mexican Hog

3   The Babiroussa

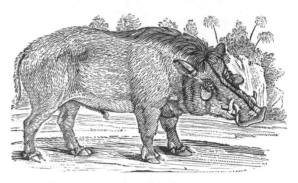

4   The African Wild Boar or Wood Swine

5   The Wild Boar

6   The Chinese Kind

7   The Common Boar

8

9

PLATE 18

1   The Cur Fox

2

3   The Greyhound Fox

4

5

6

7   The Arctic Fox

8

9

PLATE 19

2   The Wolf

1   The New South Wales Wolf

4   The Striped Hyena

3   The Spotted Hyena

6   The Jackal

5   The Racoon

PLATE 20

2

1   The Polar or Great White Bear

3

4   The Brown Bear

5

6

PLATE 21

1 The Stag or Red-Deer

2 The Elk-Antelope

3 The Grys-Bok

4 The Fallow-Deer

5 The Rein-Deer

PLATE 22

1   The Axis or Ganges Stag

2   The Elk

3   The Roe-Buck

4

5

6

7

8

PLATE 23

1   The Common Antelope

2   The Springer

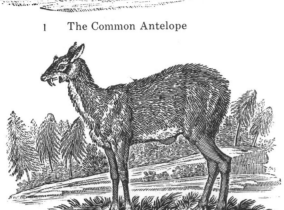

3   The Musk

4   The Gnu

5   The Chevrotain and Meminna

6   The Nyl-Ghau

7

PLATE 24

1   The Wood-Goat

2   The Hart-Beest

3   The Pied Goat

4

6

5   The American Elk

7

PLATE 25

PLATE 26

1   The Black Tiger

2   The Tiger

3   The Caracal (Lynx)

4   The Lynx

5   The Jaguar

6   The Serval

7   The Ocelot

8   The Margay or Tiger Cat

PLATE 27

1

2 The Panther

3 The Cougar

4 The Leopard

5 The Wild Cat

6 The Ounce

7

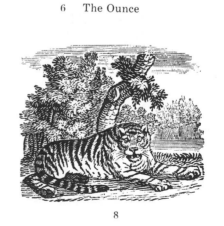

8

PLATE 28

1

2   The Elephant

3   The Two-Horned Rhinoceros

4   The Long-Nosed Tapir

5   The Rhinoceros

6   The Hippopotamus

PLATE 29

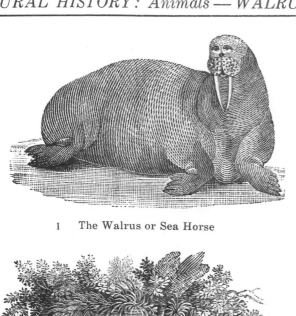

1   The Walrus or Sea Horse

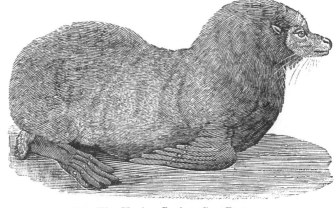

2   The Ursine Seal or Sea-Bear

3   The Otter

4   The Seal

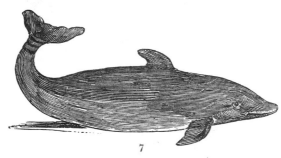

5   The Sea Otter

6

7

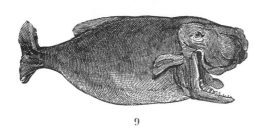

8

9

10

PLATE 30

1   The Baboon

2   The Dog-Faced Baboon

3   The Pig-Tailed Baboon

4   The Small Ribbed-Nose Baboon

5   The Striated Monkey

6   The Barbary Ape

7   The Ribbed-Nose Baboon

8   The Mico or Fair Monkey

PLATE 31

1   The Mongooz

2   The Ring-Tailed Macauco

3   The Long-Armed Ape

4   The Varied Monkey or Mona

5   The Red-Tailed Monkey

6   The Green Monkey

8

9

PLATE 32   7   The Oran-Outang

2   The Hare

1

3   The Rabbit

4

5   The Domestic Rabbit

6

8

7

9

PLATE 33

2   The Flying Squirrel

1   The Long-Tailed Squirrel

4   The Squirrel

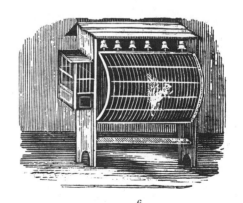

6

3   The Grey Squirrel

5   The Barbary Squirrel

7

PLATE 34

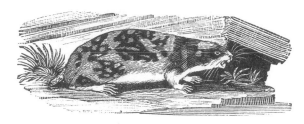

2   The Water Rat

4   The Lapland Marmot

1

3   The Quebec Marmot

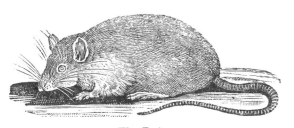

6   The Musk-Rat of Canada

5   The Marmot

8   The Rat

7   The Long-Tailed Field Mouse

9   The Mouse

PLATE 35

1   The Lesser Dormouse or Garden Squirrel

2

3   The Dormouse or Ground Squirrel

4   The Dwarf Mouse

5   The Short-Tailed Field-Mouse

6   The Hamster

7   The Muskovy Musk-Rat

8   The Souslik

9   The Tailless Marmot

PLATE 36

1   The Capibara

2   The Beaver

3   The Agouti or Long-Nosed Cavy

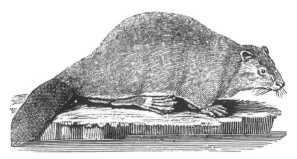

4   The Guinea-Pig or Restless Cavy

5   The Monax

6   The Jerboa

7   The Spotted Cavy

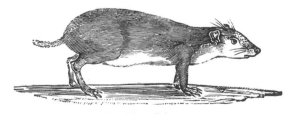

8   The Akouchi

PLATE 37

1   The Fourmart

2   The Ferret

3   The Stoat

4   The Pine-Weasel or Yellow-Breasted Martin

5   The Sable

6   The Ichneumon

7   The Weasel

8   The Fossane

PLATE 38

1 The Badger

2 The Ratel

3 The Wolverine or Glutton

4 The Skunk

5 The Suricate or Four-Toed Weasel

6 The Coati or Brazilian Weasel

7 The Zibet

8 The Genet

9 The Civet

PLATE 39

1   The Spotted Opossum of New South Wales

2   The Phalanger

3   The Kangaroo

4   The Kangaroo Rat of New South Wales

5   The Opossum of Van Diemen's Land

PLATE 40

1   The Squirrel Opossum

2   The Saragoy   3   The Murine

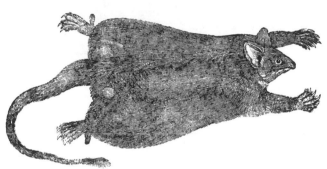

4   The Wombach

5   The Mexican Opossum

6   The Flying Opossum of New South Wales

PLATE 41

1   The Ant-Eater

2   The Great Manis

3   The Nine-Banded Armadillo

4   The Six-Banded Armadillo

5   The Sloth

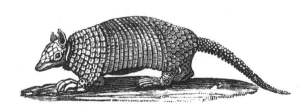

6   The Kabassou

PLATE 42

1   The Radiated Mole

2   The Mole

3   The Water Shrew Mouse

4   The Shrew Mouse

5   The Tanrec

6   The Tendrac

PLATE 43

1. The Brazilian Porcupine

2. The Porcupine

4. The Canada Porcupine

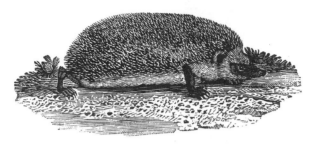

3. The Hedge-Hog or Urchin

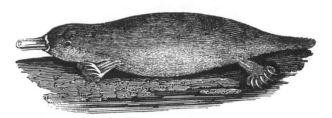

5. The Platypus

PLATE 44

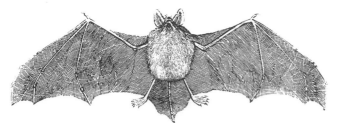

1 The Short-Eared Bat

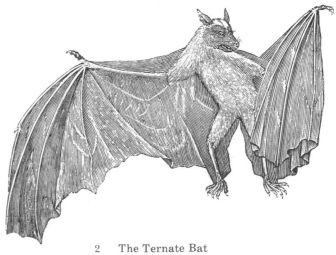

2 The Ternate Bat

3 The Long-Eared Bat

4 The Turtle

5 The Frog

6 The Brazilian Chameleon

PLATE 45

1   The Spotted Flycatcher

2   The Nuthatch

3   The Pied Flycatcher

4   The Pied Flycatcher

5   The Swallow

6   The Sand Martin

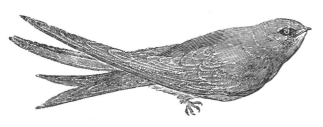

7   The Swift

8   The Martin

PLATE 46

1   The Hedge Warbler

2   The Redstart

3   The Grasshopper Warbler

4   The Passerine Warbler

5   The Dartford Warbler

6   The Reed Warbler

7   The Chiff Chaff

PLATE 47

1   The Water Ouzel

2   The Grey Wagtail

3   The Pied Wagtail

4   The Yellow Wagtail

5   The Greater Redpole

6   The Anthus Richardi

7   The Lesser Redpole

PLATE 48

1   The Siskin

2   The Linnet

3   The Goldfinch

4   The Sparrow

5   The Bullfinch

6   The Mountain Sparrow

7   The Mountain Linnet

8   The Mountain Finch

PLATE 49

1   The Grosbeak

2   The Parrot Cross-Bill

3   The Cross-Bill

4   The Grosbeak

5   The Green Grosbeak

PLATE 50

1   The Golden-Crested Wren

2   The Willow Wren

3   The Yellow Wren

4   The Redbreast

5   The Least Willow Wren

6   The Wren

7   The Black-Cap

PLATE 51

1   The Black-Headed Bunting

2   The Yellow Bunting

3   The Cirl Bunting

4   The Snow Bunting

5   The Tawny Bunting

6   The Green-Headed Bunting

7   The Bunting

PLATE 52

1   The Bearded Titmouse

2   The Crested Titmouse

3   The Blue Titmouse

4   The Marsh Titmouse

5   The Coal Titmouse

6   The Long-Tailed Titmouse

7   The Titmouse

PLATE 53

1   The Woodchat

2   The Stonechat

3   The White-Throat

4   The Wheatear

5   The Woodchat

6   The Whinchat

7   The Lesser White-Throat

PLATE 54

1   The Tree Lark

2   The Lark

3   The Field Lark

4   The Titlark

5   The Woodlark

PLATE 55

1   The Missel Thrush

2   The Throstle

3   The Fieldfare

4   The Redwing

PLATE 56

1   The Turtle Dove

2   The Nightingale

3   The Wild Pigeon

4   The Chatterer

5   The Ring Dove

PLATE 57

1   The Ash-Coloured Shrike

2   The Red-Backed Shrike

3   The Golden Oriole

4   The Fork-Tailed Indian Shrike

PLATE 58

1   The Raven

2   The Jack-Daw

3   The Blackbird

4

5   The Rook

6   The Hooded Crow

PLATE 59

1   The Chough

2   The Rose Coloured Starling or Thrush

3   The Nutcracker

4   The Starling

5   The Crested Grackle

6   The Brown Starling

PLATE 60

1   The Magpie

2   The Jay

3   The Ring Ouzel

4   The Silky Starling

5   The Mino

PLATE 61

1   The Bee Eater

2   The Night-Jar

3   The Cuckoo

4   The Kingfisher

5   The Hoopoe

6   The Roller

PLATE 62

1   The White-Tailed Eagle

2   The Ringtailed Eagle

3   The Golden Eagle

4   The Sea Eagle

PLATE 63

1   The Sparrowhawk

2   The Goshawk

3   The Little Black and Orange Coloured Indian Hawk

4   The Bearded Vulture

5   The Crested Vulture

6

PLATE 64

1   The Buzzard

2   The Moor Buzzard

3   The Ash Coloured Buzzard

4   The Honey Buzzard

PLATE 65

1   The Kestrel

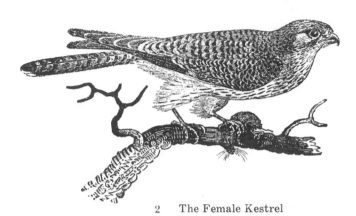

2   The Female Kestrel

3   The Secretary

4

5   The Ringtail

6

7

PLATE 66

2   The Stone Falcon

1   The Hen-Harrier

4   The Ash Coloured Falcon

3   The Jer-Falcon

6   The Rough-Legged Falcon

5   Peregrine Falcon

PLATE 67

1   The Hobby

2   The Merlin

3   The Osprey

4

5

6   The Kite

7

PLATE 68

2   The Snowy Owl

1   The Eagle Owl

4   The Little Owl

3   The Female Short-Eared Owl

5

PLATE 69

1   The Short-Eared Owl

2   The Tawny Owl

3   The Long-Eared Owl

4   The Yellow Owl

5   The Scops Eared Owl

PLATE 70

1   The Red-Breasted Goose

2   The Shieldrake

3   The Bernacle

4   The White-Fronted Wild Goose

5   The Tame Duck

6   The Scoter

PLATE 71

1   The Eider Duck

2

3   The Mallard

4   The Gadwall

5   The Scaup Duck

6   The Long-Tailed Duck

7   The Common Duck

PLATE 72

1   The Wigeon

2   The Spur-Winged Goose

3   The Garganey

4   The Bimaculated Duck

5   The Velvet Duck

6   The Golden-Eye

7   The Pochard

8

PLATE 73

1   The King Duck

2   The Pintail Duck

3   The Teal

4

5

6   The Ferruginous Duck

7   The Muskovy Duck

8   The Castaneous Duck

9   The Tufted Duck

PLATE 74

1 The Cravat Goose

2 The Swan Goose

3 The Tame Goose

4 The Brent Goose

5 The Shoveler

6 The Grey Lag Goose

PLATE 75

1   The Lough Diver

2   The Smew

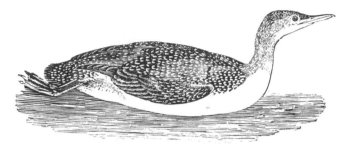

3   The Second Speckled Diver

4   The Dun-Diver

5   The Goosander

PLATE 76

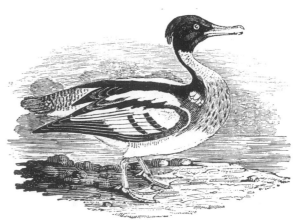

1   The Black-Throated Diver

2   The Red-Breasted Merganser

4   The First Speckled Diver

3   The Great Northern Diver

5   The Red-Throated Diver

PLATE 77

1

2

3

4

5

PLATE 78

1   The Domestic Cock

2   The Turkey

3   The Pintado (Guinea Fowl)

4   The Judcock (Jacksnipe)

5

6

7

8

PLATE 79

1   The Red-Legged Partridge

2   The Great Snipe

3   The Woodcock

4   The Snipe

5   The Quail

6   The Partridge

PLATE 80

1   The White Grouse

2   The Wood Grouse

3   The Black Grouse

4   The Pheasant

5   The Red Grouse

PLATE 81

2   The Green Woodpecker

1   The Black Woodpecker

4   The Pied Woodpecker

3   The Barred Woodpecker

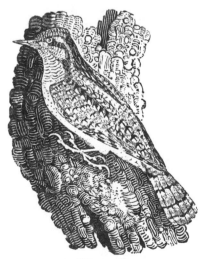

5   The Three-Toed Woodpecker

6   The Wryneck

PLATE 82

1

2

3   The Peacock

4   The Sapphire Crowned Paroquet

5   The Ring Paroquet

6   The Little Guinea Paroquet

7   The Golden Winged Paroquet

PLATE 83

1   The Green Sandpiper

2   The Common Sandpiper

3   The Red-Legged Sandpiper

4   The Spotted Sandpiper

5   The Selninger Sandpiper

PLATE 84

1   The Turnstone

2   The Knot

3   The Red Sandpiper

4   The Wood Sandpiper

5   The Turnstone

6   The Lapwing

PLATE 85

1   The Scolopax Sabini

2   The Pratincole

3   The Dunlin

4   The Sanderling

5   The Little Stint

6   The Purre (Dunlin in winter plumage)

PLATE 86

1   The Ruff

2   The Great Plover

3   The Golden Plover

4   The Grey Plover

5   The Ring Dotterel

6   The Dotterel

PLATE 87

1   The Spotted Rail or Spotted Gallinule

2   The Common Gallinule

3   The Water Rail

4   The Little Gallinule

5   The Olivaceous Gallinule

6   The Land-Rail or Corn-Crake

PLATE 88

1   The Curlew

2   The Whimbrel

3   The Redshank

4   The Spotted Redshank

5   The Greenshank

6   The Pigmy Curlew

PLATE 89

2   The Red Godwit

1   The Great Bustard

3   The Godwit

4   The Little Bustard

5   The Cinereous Godwit

PLATE 90

1   The Oyster-Catcher

2   The Crane

3   The Spoonbill

4   The Glossy Ibis

5   The Avoset

6   The Long-Legged Plover

PLATE 91

1   The Buff-Coloured Egret

2   The Little Egret

3   The Little Bittern

4

5

6   The Stork

7

8

PLATE 92

2   The Night Heron

1   The Bittern

4   The Little White Heron

3   The Heron

5   The Female Little Bittern

PLATE 93

1   The Lesser Black-Backed Gull

2   The Young Glaucous Gull

3   The Black-Backed Gull

4   The Glaucous Gull

5

6   The Arctic Gull

PLATE 94

1   The Young Kittiwake

2   The Herring Gull

3   The Black Tern

4   The Shearwater

5   The Sandwich Tern

6   The Roseate Tern

PLATE 95

1   The Skua Gull

2   The Common Gull

3   The Ivory Gull

4   The Fulmar

5   The Red-Legged Gull

6   The Lesser Tern

PLATE 96

1   The Kittiwake

2   The Black-Headed Gull

3   The Wagel (Gull)

4   The Black-Toed Gull

5   The Common Tern

PLATE 97

1   The Lesser Guillemot

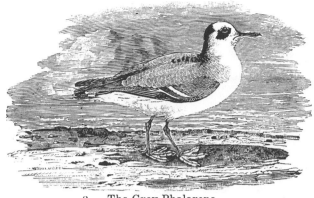

2   The Grey Phalarope

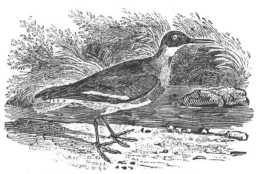

3   The Red Necked Phalarope

4   The Red Phalarope

5   The Fork-Tailed Petrel

6   The Stormy Petrel

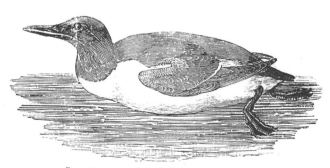

7   The Foolish Guillemot

8   The Black Guillemot

PLATE 98

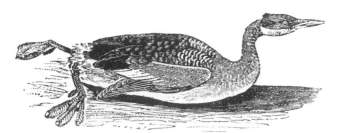

1   The Red-Necked Grebe

2   The Eared Grebe

3   The Little Grebe

5   The Tippet Grebe

4   The Coot

6   The Dusky Grebe

7   The Great-Crested Grebe

PLATE 99

1   The Crested Cormorant

2   The Cormorant

3   The Lesser Imber

4   The Shag

PLATE 100

1   The Razor-Bill

2   The Black-Billed Auk

3   The Great Auk

4   The Gannet (Sea Fowl)

5   The Little Auk

6   The Puffin

PLATE 101

PLATE 102

PLATE 103

1

2

3

4

5

6

7

8

9

PLATE 104

PLATE 105

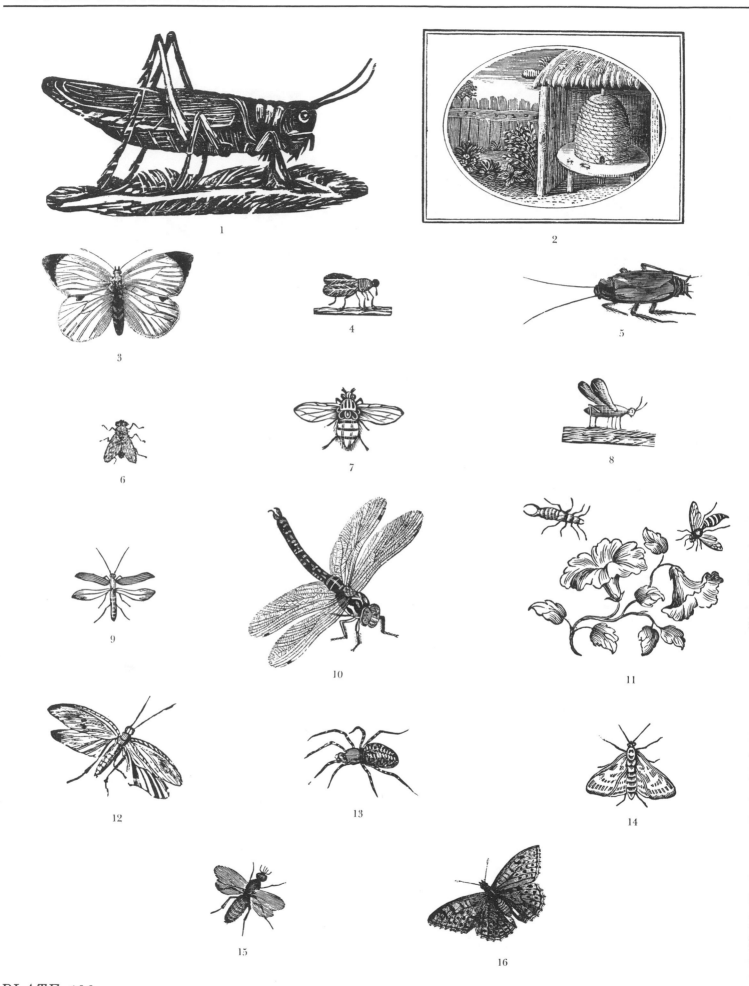

PLATE 106

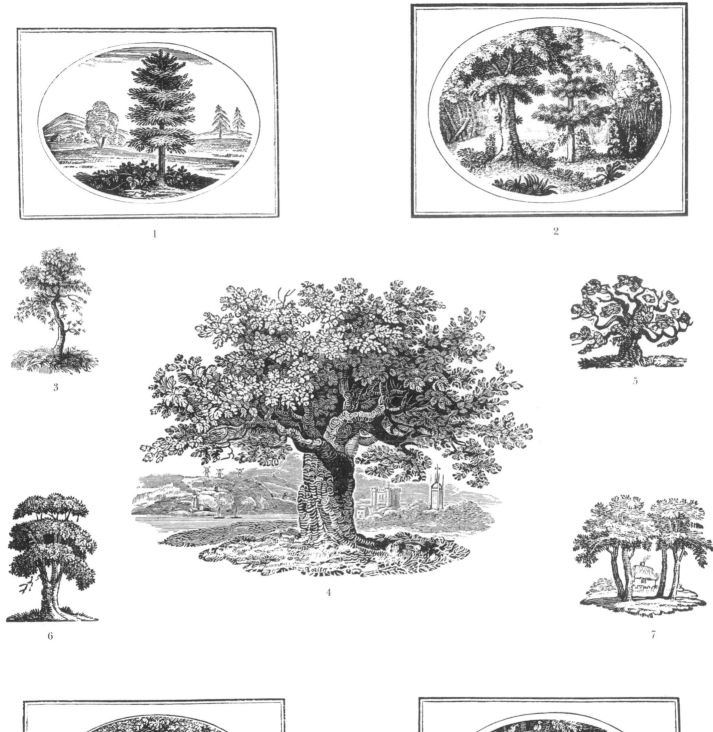

1

2

3

4

5

6

7

8

9

PLATE 107

1

2

3

4

5

6

7

8

9

PLATE 108

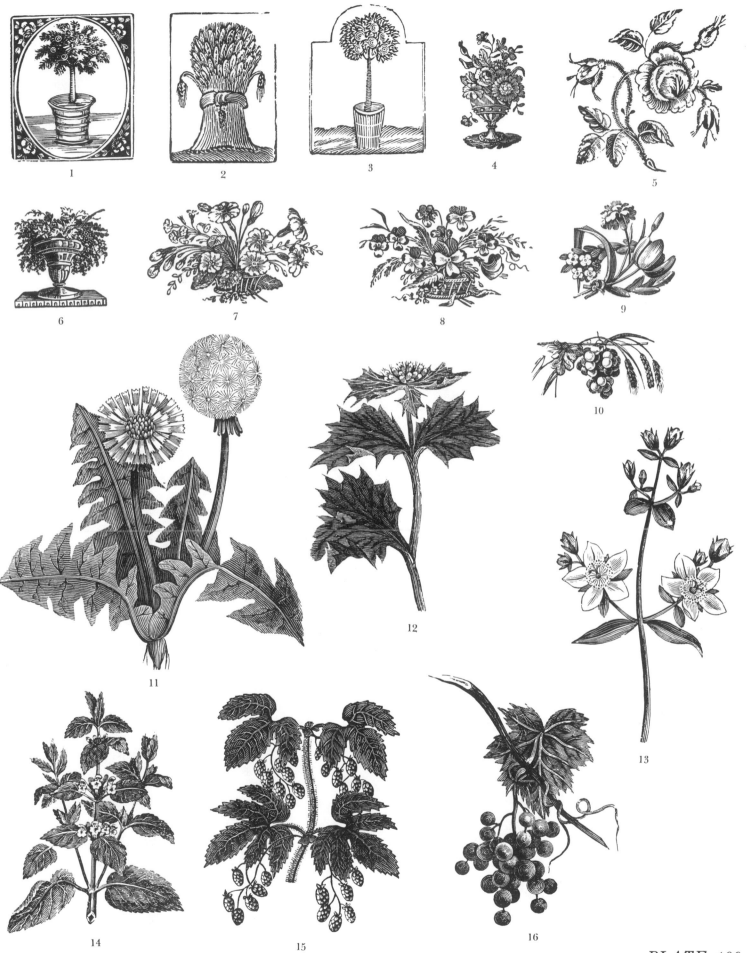

1

2

3

4

5

6

7

8

9

10

11

12

13

14

15

16

PLATE 109

1

2

3

4

5

6

7

8

9

10

PLATE 110

1

2

3

4

5

6

PLATE 111

1

2

3

4

5

6

7

8

9

10

PLATE 112

PEOPLE

1

2

3

4

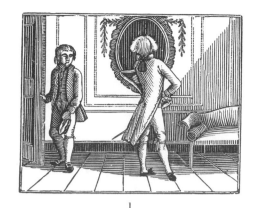

5

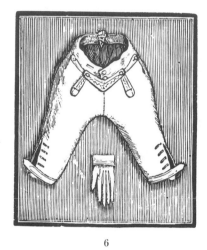

6

7

8

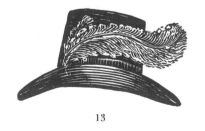

9

10

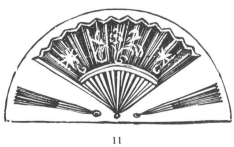

11

12

13

PLATE 113

1

2

3

4

5

6

7

PLATE 114

1

2

3

4

5

6

7

8

9

PLATE 115

1

2

3

4

5

6

7

8

PLATE 116

PLATE 117

1

2

3

4

5

6

7

PLATE 118

1

2

3

4

5

6

7

8

9

PLATE 119

1

2

3

4

5

6

7

PLATE 120

1

2

3

4

5

6

7

8

PLATE 121

PLATE 122

1

2

3

4

5

6

7

8

9

10

PLATE 123

PLATE 124

PLATE 125

1

2

3

4

5

6

7

PLATE 126

PLATE 127

1

2

3

4

5

6

7

8

PLATE 128

1

2

3

4

5

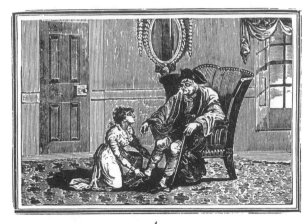

6

7

PLATE 129

1

2

3

4

5

6

7

8

PLATE 130

PLATE 131

PLATE 132

1

2

3

4

5

6

7

8

9

PLATE 133

1

2

3

4

5

6

7

PLATE 134

1

2

3

4

5

6

7

8

9

10

11

12

PLATE 135

PLATE 136

1

2

3

4

5

6

7

8

9

10

PLATE 137

PLATE 138

1

2

3

4

5

6

7

8

9

PLATE 139

1

2

3

4

5

PLATE 140

PLATE 141

PLATE 142

PLATE 143

1

2

3

4

5

6

7

PLATE 144

1

2

3

4

5

6

7

8

9

10

PLATE 145

PLATE 146

1

2

3

4

5

6

7

8

9

10

11

PLATE 147

1

2

3

4

5

6

7

8

9

PLATE 148

PLATE 149

PLATE 150

1

2

3

4

5

6

7

PLATE 151

1

2

3

4

6

7

5

8

9

10

PLATE 152

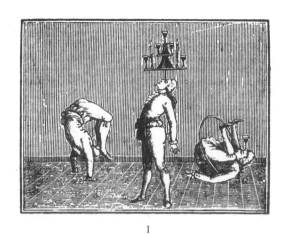

1

3

4

5

6

2

7

PLATE 153

1

2

3

4

5

6

7

PLATE 154

1

2

3

4

5

6

7

8

9

PLATE 155

MR KINLOCH'S BALL.

MASQUERADE
at the Assembly Rooms
Newcastle

1

2

3

4

5

6

7

8

9

PLATE 156

1

2

3

4

5

6

7

8

9

PLATE 157

1

2

3

4

5

6

7

PLATE 158

1   Fire

2   Deluge

3   Fire

4   Famine

5   Earthquake

PLATE 159

1

2

4

3

5

6

PLATE 160

1

2

3

4

5

6

7

8

PLATE 161

1

2

3

4

5

6

7

8

PLATE 162

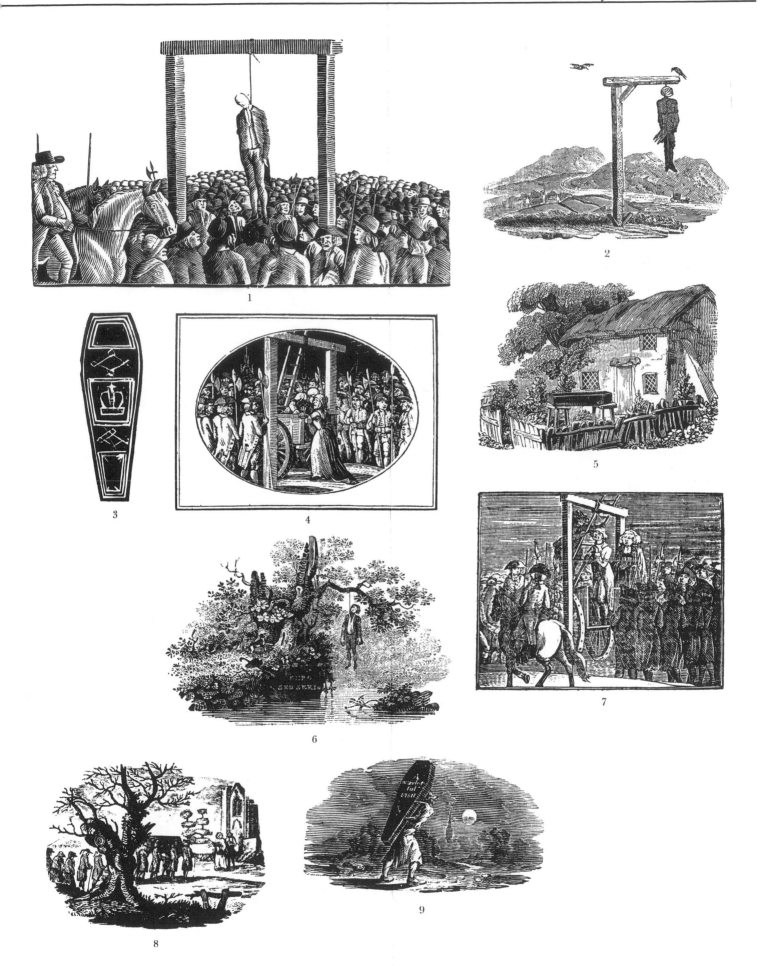

PLATE 163

1

2

3

4

5

6

7

8

9

10

11

12

PLATE 164

BUSINESS & TRADES

1

2

3

4

5

6

7

PLATE 165

1

2

3

4

5

6

7

8

PLATE 166

1

2

3

4

5

6

7

8

9

PLATE 167

PLATE 168

PLATE 169

1

2

3

4

5

6

7

8

9

PLATE 170

6

9

2

4

1

3

5

7

8

PLATE 171

1 Baker

2 Blacksmith

3 Vineyard

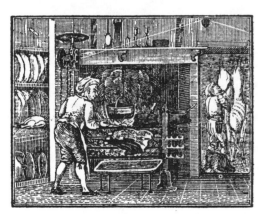

4 Butcher and Cook

5 Brewer

6 Woodcutter

7

8 Blacksmith

9 Woodcutter

PLATE 172

1   Auctioneer

2   Delivery Boy

3   Tailor

4   Shopkeeper

5   Shoe-Maker

6   Shopkeeper

7   Delivery Boy

8   Auctioneer

PLATE 173

1 Cooper

2 Glass-Blower

3 Coach-Maker

4 Cabinet-Maker

5 Brick-Maker

6 Builder

7 Potter

8 Tanner and Currier

PLATE 174

1   Weaver

2   Turner

3   Salt-Pans

4   Mills

5   Mining

6   Mining

7   Paper-Maker

8   Forge

PLATE 175

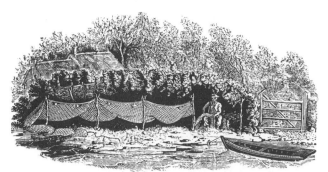

1 Fishermen

2 Turner

3 Printer

4 Fishermen

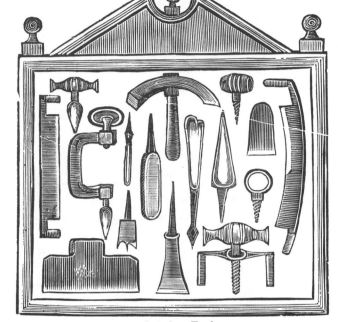

6 Leather Tools

5 Printer

7 Lye

8 Wheelmaker

9 Water Cart

PLATE 176

1 Sculpture

2 Painting

3 Art Dealer

4 Teaching

5 Astronomy

PLATE 177

1   Gooseberries

2   Rosemary and Sweetbriar

3   Dumpling Woman

4   Hot Cross Buns

5   Kitchen Stuff Maids

6   Lavender

7   Shirt Buttons

8   White Radish, Lettuce

9   New Whiting

10 Strawberry Woman

11 New Cockles

12 New Salmon

PLATE 178

1   Buy Great Smelts

2   Flowers, Cut Flowers

3   Buy Great Mussels

4   Buy Great Eels

5   Herb-Wife

6   Strawberries Ripe and
     Cherries in the Rise

7   Flowers

8   Fine Ripe Oranges

9   Fresh Fish

PLATE 179

1   Chimney Sweepers

2   Cucumbers

3

4   Mat, a Mill-Mat

5

6   Water Carrier

7   Old Shoes for Brooms

8   Old Clowze, Any Old Clo', Clo'

9   Small Coals Here

10   Any Old Iron Take Money For?

11   Old Cloaks, Suits or Coats

PLATE 180

Potatoes, Kidney Potatoes

2   Capers, Anchovies

3

4   Marking Stone

5   Tinker

6

7   Buy a Mouse Trap

8   St. Thomas Onions

9

10   Rabbit Man

11   Banbury Cakes

12

PLATE 181

1

2

3

4

PLATE 182

1

2

3

4

5

6

7

8

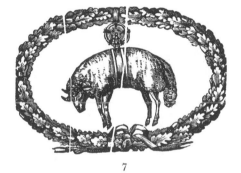

9

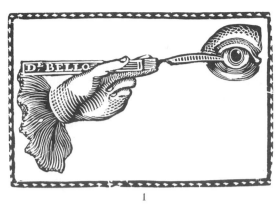

10

11

12

PLATE 183

1

2

3

4

5

6

7

8

9

10

PLATE 184

PLATE 185

1

2

3

4

5

6

7

8

9

10

11

12

PLATE 186

1

2

3

4

5

6

7

PLATE 187

PLATE 188

PLATE 189

PLATE 190

PLATE 191

1

2

3

4

5

6

7

8

PLATE 192

PLATE 193

1

2

3

4

5

6

PLATE 194

1

2

3

4

5

6

7

8

9

10

PLATE 195

1

2

3

4

5

6

7

8

PLATE 196

PLATE 197

1

2

3

4

PLATE 198

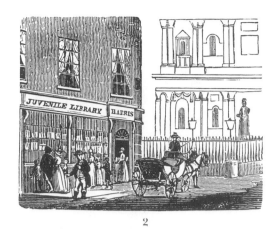

1

2

3

4

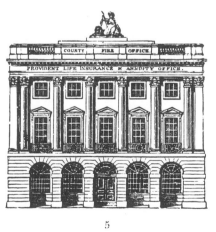

5

PLATE 199

PLATE 200

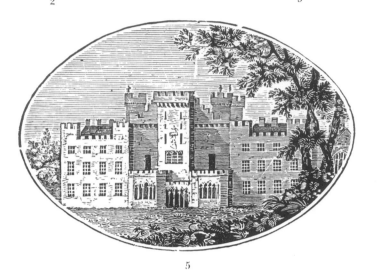

1

2

3

4

5

6

7

PLATE 201

1

2

3

4

5

6

7

PLATE 202

1

2

3

4

5

6

PLATE 203

1

2

3

4

5

6

7

PLATE 204

JAMES the II.

1683

PLATE 205

GRAPHIC ARTS

1

2

3

4

5

6

7

8

9

PLATE 206

1 Edward II   2 Stephen   3 Edward III

4 Henry IV   5 William the Conqueror   6 Henry VIII

7 Charles II   8 George I   9 James II

10 Mary   11 Henry VI   12 James I

PLATE 207

PLATE 208

Ape | Bear | Magpye | Nag

Cow | Dog | Ounce | Plover

Elke | Fox | Quail | Ruff

Goat | Hare | Snipe | Teal

Ibex | Jay | Unicorn | Weefil

Kite | Lion | Yellow hammer | Zebra

1

2

3

4

PLATE 209

1

2

3

4

b Bull | c Cat
d Dog | e Egg | f Fiſh
g Goat | h Hog | J Judge
K King | l Lion | m Mouſe
n Nag | o Owl | p Peacock
q Queen | r Robin | ſ Squirrel
t Top | v Vine | w Whale
x Xerxes | y young Lamb | z Zani

A Ape. a | B Bear. b
C Cock. c | D Dog. d
E Elephant. e | F Fox. f
G Goose. g | H Horse h
J Ibex i | K King-fisher. k

PLATE 210

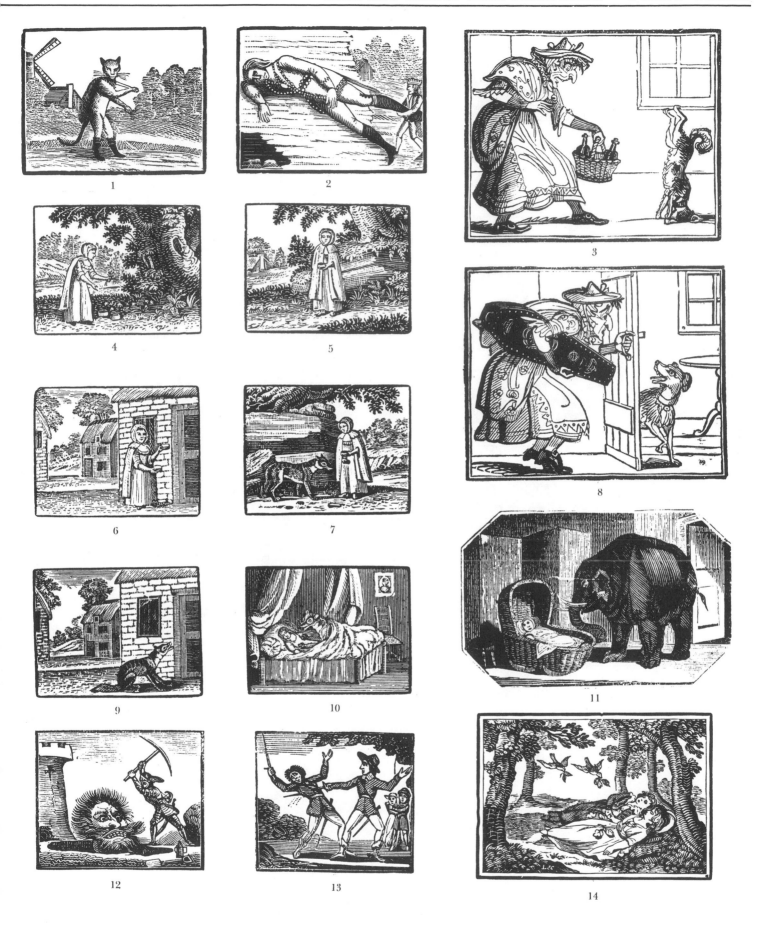

1

2

3

4

5

6

7

8

9

10

11

12

13

14

PLATE 211

1   2

3   4

5   6

7

PLATE 212

1

2

3

4

5

6

7

PLATE 213

1

2

3

4

5

6

7

PLATE 214

PLATE 215

1

2

3

4

5

6

PLATE 216

PLATE 217

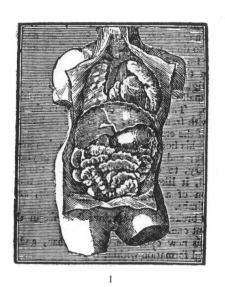

1

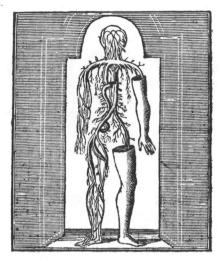

2

3

4

5

6

PLATE *218*

PLATE 219

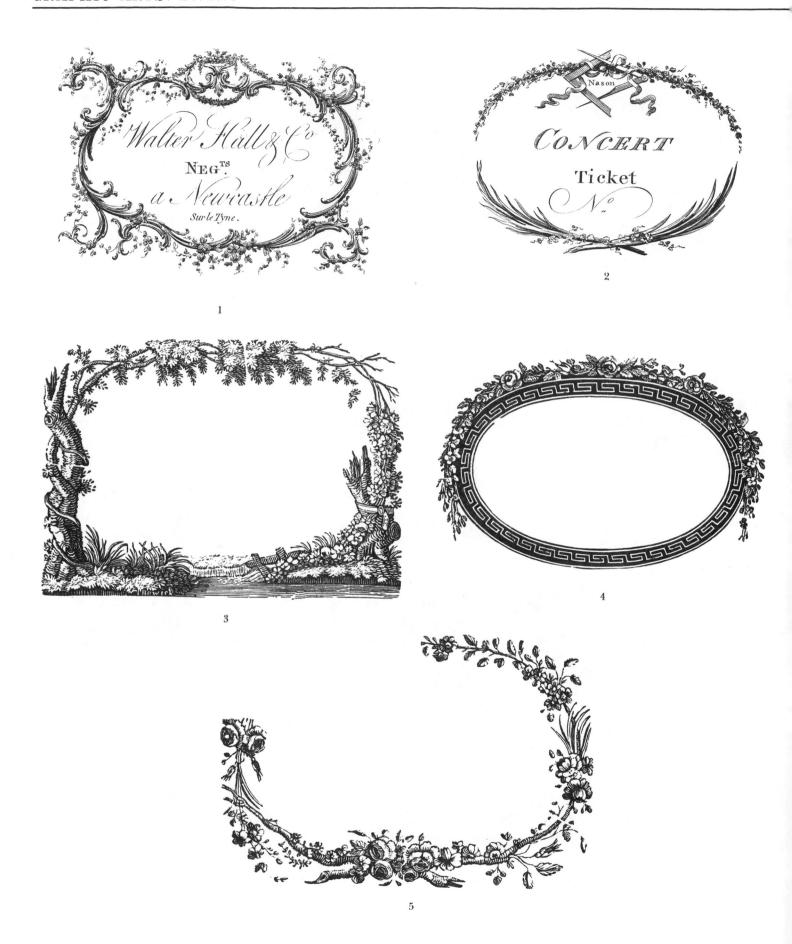

PLATE 220

PLATE 221

PLATE 222

1

2

3

4

5

6

7

8

PLATE 223

PLATE 224

PLATE 225

1

2

3

4

5

6

7

8

9

10

11

12

13

14

PLATE 226

1

2

3

4

5

6

7

8

9

10

11

12

13

14

PLATE 227

PLATE 228

PLATE 229

BIBLIOGRAPHY

The illustrations used in this book were extracted from the works listed in this Bibliography. Each book has been assigned a brief code identification; this code is used in the Sources of Plates to indicate the original source of all illustrations.

Code

BBa Bewick, Thomas. *A History of British Birds. Vol. I.* Containing the History and Description of Land Birds. London: Longman and Co., 1826.

BBb Bewick, Thomas. *A History of British Birds. Vol. II.* Containing the History and Description of Water Birds. London: Longman and Co., 1826.

BEa Bell, J. G. *Scrapbook of Thomas Bewick. Woodcuts. Book I.* London: circa 1870.

BEb Bell, J. G. *Scrapbook of Thomas Bewick. Woodcuts. Book II.* London: circa 1870.

Code

BIa Bewick, Thomas. *A History of British Birds. Vol. 1.* Containing the History and Description of Land Birds. London: Longman and Co., 1797.

BIb Bewick, Thomas. *A History of British Birds. Vol. 2.* Containing the History and Description of Water Birds. London: Longman, 1797.

BOa Boyd, Julia (ed.). *Bewick Gleanings: Being Impressions from Copperplates and Wood Block Engravings in the Bewick Workshop. Part I.* Newcastle-upon-Tyne: Andrew Reid, 1886.

231

Code

BOb   Boyd, Julia (ed.). *Bewick Gleanings: Being Impressions from Copperplates and Wood Block Engravings in the Bewick Workshop. Part II.* Newcastle-upon-Tyne: Andrew Reid, 1886.

BP   Melmoth, Sidney (ed.). *Beauties of British Poetry.* Second edition. London: Brook and Lancashire, 1803.

BU   Burns, Robert. *The Poetical Works of Robert Burns; With His Life. Ornamented with Engravings on Wood by Mr. Bewick, from Original Designs by Mr. Thurston.* 2 vols. Alnwick: Catnach and Davison, 1808.

CR   Hindley, Charles. *A History of the Cries of London, Ancient and Modern. Woodcuts by Thomas and John Bewick and Their Pupils.* London: Reeves and Turner, 1881.

CU   Leadenhall Press (ed.). *1,000 Quaint Cuts.* London: Field and Tuer, The Leadenhall Press, E. C., undated.

D   Dobson, Austin. *Thomas Bewick and His Pupils.* London: Chatto and Windus, 1889.

FA   Bewick, Thomas and John. *Select Fables; With Cuts, Designed and Engraved by Thomas and John Bewick, and Others, Previous to the Year 1784: Together with a Memoir; and a Descriptive Catalogue of the Works of Messrs. Bewick.* London: Emerson Charnley and Baldwin, Cradock, and Joy, 1820.

FB   Bloomfield, Robert. *The Farmer's Boy; A Rural Poem.* Fourteenth edition. London: Longman, Hurst, Rees, Orme, and Brown; Baldwin, Cradock, and Joy; Darton, Harvey, and Co.; G. Cowie and Co., and Edwards and Knibb, 1820.

Code

H   Hugo, Thomas. *Bewick's Woodcuts: Impressions of Upwards of Two Thousand Wood-Blocks, Engraved, For the Most Part, by Thomas and John Bewick, of Newcastle-on-Tyne.* London: L. Reeve and Co., 1870.

HS   Bewick, Thomas. *A General History of Quadrupeds.* London: Longman, Hurst, Rees, Orme, and Brown, 1811.

L   Bewick, John. *The Looking-Glass for the Mind. Cuts Designed and Engraved by (John) Bewick.* London: E. Newberry, 1792.

M   Bewick, Thomas. *A Memoir of Thomas Bewick, Written by Himself. Embellished by Numerous Wood Engravings, Designed and Engraved by the Author for a Work on British Fishes, and Never Before Published.* London: Longman, Green, Longman, and Roberts, 1862.

P   Trusler, John, Rev. Dr. *The Progress of Man and Society. Illustrated by Upwards of One Hundred and Twenty Cuts.* London: John Trusler, 1791.

Q   Bewick, Thomas. *The Figures of Bewick's Quadrupeds.* Second edition. Newcastle: Edward Walker, 1824.

R   Robinson, Robert. *Thomas Bewick: His Life and Times.* Newcastle: R. Robinson, 1867.

SP   Mavor, William. *The English Spelling Book.* Alnwick: undated.

SU   Hugo, Thomas. *The Bewick Collector. A Supplement to a Descriptive Catalogue of the Works of Thomas and John Bewick.* London: L. Reeve and Co., 1868.

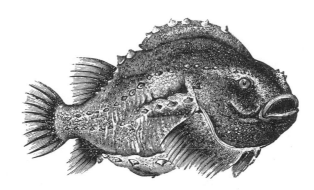

APPENDIX: *Sources of Plates*

(See the Bibliography for full identification of code symbols)

Plate

1: 1 through 7—Q
2: 1 through 6—Q; 7—R; 8 through 10—Q
3: 1 through 8—Q
4: 1, 2—H; 3 through 5—FA; 6, 7—H; 8, 9—BBa; 10—FA; 11 through 13—H
5: 1—H; 2—Q; 3—HS; 4—H; 5, 6—FA; 7—BOb; 8—H; 9—BBa; 10—H
6: 1—H; 2 through 8—Q
7: 1—BBa; 2 through 4—H; 5—FA; 6—H; 7—R; 8—H
8: 1 through 9—H
9: 1, 2—Q; 3, 4—H; 5, 6—FA
10: 1 through 4—Q
11: 1—R
12: 1 through 8—Q
13: 1—H; 2—FA; 3—H; 4—FB; 5, 6—H; 7—Q; 8, 9—H; 10—BBb; 11—H; 12—BBa; 13—H
14: 1 through 5—Q

Plate

15: 1 through 6—Q; 7—H
16: 1 through 6—Q
17: 1 through 4—Q; 5—FA; 6—Q; 7—BU; 8—BOb
18: 1 through 7—Q; 8—BBa; 9—H
19: 1—Q; 2—H; 3—Q; 4 through 6—FA; 7—Q; 8, 9—H
20. 1 through 6—Q
21: 1, 2—Q; 3—H; 4—Q; 5, 6—FA
22: 1 through 5—Q
23: 1 through 3—Q; 4—FA; 5—BOa; 6—H; 7, 8—FA
24: 1 through 6—Q; 7—H
25: 1 through 3—Q; 4—FA; 5—Q; 6—FA; 7—H
26: 1—Q; 2, 3—H; 4 through 6—FA
27: 1 through 8—Q
28: 1—H; 2 through 6—Q; 7, 8—FA
29: 1—HS; 2 through 6—Q

Plate

30: 1 through 5—Q; 6—HS; 7 through 10—H
31: 1 through 8—Q
32: 1 through 7—Q; 8, 9—HS
33: 1 through 3—Q; 4—FA; 5—Q; 6—H; 7—FA; 8—H; 9—BBa
34: 1 through 5—Q; 6—FA; 7—HS
35: 1 through 8—Q; 9—BOb
36: 1 through 9—Q
37: 1 through 8—Q
38: 1 through 8—Q
39: 1 through 9—Q
40: 1 through 5—Q
41: 1 through 6—Q
42: 1 through 6—Q
43: 1 through 6—Q
44: 1 through 5—Q
45: 1 through 3—Q; 4—FA; 5, 6—H
46: 1 through 5—BBa; 6—BIa; 7, 8—BBa
47: 1 through 7—BBa
48: 1 through 7—BBa
49: 1 through 8—BBa
50: 1 through 5—BBa
51: 1—BBa; 2—BIb; 3 through 7—BBa
52: 1 through 7—BBa
53: 1 through 7—BBa
54: 1 through 7—BBa
55: 1 through 5—BBa
56: 1 through 4—BBa
57: 1 through 3—BBa; 4—BIb; 5—BBa
58: 1 through 3—BBa; 4—BBb
59: 1 through 6—BBa
60: 1 through 6—BBa
61: 1 through 5—BBa
62: 1 through 3—BBa; 4—BBb; 5, 6—BBa
63: 1 through 4—BBa
64: 1 through 4—BBa; 5—BBb; 6—BBa
65: 1—BBa; 2—BBb; 3—BBb; 4—BBa
66: 1—BBa; 2—BIb; 3—BBa; 4—H; 5—BBa; 6, 7—FA
67: 1 through 6—BBa
68: 1 through 3—BBa; 4, 5—FA; 6—BBa; 7—FA
69: 1 through 5—BBa
70: 1 through 5—BBa
71: 1 through 6—BBb
72: 1—BBb; 2—FA; 3 through 6—BBb; 7—D
73: 1 through 7—BBb; 8—FA
74: 1 through 4—BBb; 5—BBa; 6 through 9—BBb
75: 1 through 6—BBb
76: 1 through 5—BBb
77: 1 through 5—BBb
78: 1, 2—BBb; 3 through 5—H
79: 1—BIb; 2 through 4—BIa; 5—FA; 6—H; 7, 8—FA
80: 1—BBa; 2 through 4—BBb; 5, 6—BBa
81: 1 through 5—BBa
82: 1 through 4—BBa; 5—BBb; 6—BBa
83: 1, 2—FA; 3 through 7—BBb
84: 1 through 5—BBb
85: 1 through 6—BBb
86: 1—BBb; 2—BBa; 3—BBb; 4—BBa; 5—BIb; 6—BBb
87: 1, 2—BBb; 3—BBa; 4—BBb; 5, 6—BBa
88: 1 through 6—BBb
89: 1 through 6—BBb
90: 1—BBa; 2, 3—BBb; 4—BBa; 5—BBb
91: 1 through 5—BBb; 6—BBa

Plate

92: 1 through 3—BBb; 4, 5—FA; 6—BBb; 7—BBa; 8—L
93: 1 through 5—BBb
94: 1 through 6—BBb
95: 1 through 6—BBb
96: 1 through 6—BBb
97: 1 through 5—BBb
98: 1 through 8—BBb
99: 1 through 7—BBb
100: 1 through 4—BBb
101: 1 through 6—BBb
102: 1, 2—FA; 3 through 5—H; 6, 7—FA; 8, 9—H; 10, 11—FA; 12, 13—H; 14, 15—FA; 16—H
103: 1—BBa; 2—BOa; 3, 4—FA; 5—H; 6—BU; 7, 8—BBa; 9, 10—FA; 11—BBa; 12—H; 13—FA; 14, 15—BBa; 16—L
104: 1 through 3—M; 4—FA; 5—M; 6—FA; 7, 8—M; 9—FA
105: 1 through 6—M; 7, 8—H; 9 through 11—M
106: 1—H; 2, 3—FA; 4, 5—H; 6—HS; 7 through 9—H; 10—FA; 11 through 15—H; 16—FA
107: 1, 2—FA; 3, 4—R; 5, 6—H; 7—HS; 8, 9—FA
108: 1—BOa; 2—FA; 3 through 7—H; 8, 9—FA
109: 1 through 16—H
110: 1 through 4—BBb; 5—FA; 6 through 9—BBb; 10—BP
111: 1—FA; 2—R; 3 through 6—BBb
112: 1—HS; 2—BBa; 3—HS; 4—P; 5—H; 6 through 8—BBa; 9—FB; 10—BBa
113: 1 through 13—H
114: 1 through 7—H
115: 1—H; 2—FA; 3—H; 4—BOa; 5—H; 6—BBb; 7 through 9—BBa
116: 1—H; 2—HS; 3—BBb; 4, 5—FA; 6—H; 7, 8—BBb
117: 1—BBa; 2—R; 3—BBa; 4—H; 5, 6—FA; 7—H; 8—BBa
118: 1 through 3—HS; 4, 5—P; 6—BBa; 7—HS
119: 1—P; 2—BEa; 3—L; 4, 5—HS; 6—BBa; 7—BU; 8—BBa; 9—HS
120: 1—H; 2, 3—CU; 4—H; 5—P; 6, 7—CU
121: 1, 2—L; 3—H; 4, 5—L; 6—CU; 7, 8—L
122: 1 through 3—H; 4—L; 5—H; 6—L; 7—H; 8—FA
123: 1 through 4—BBa; 5—L; 6—P; 7—H; 8—BOa; 9—BBa; 10—H
124: 1—H; 2—R; 3—H; 4—R; 5—H; 6—L; 7—R; 8—P; 9—L; 10—H; 11—L
125: 1, 2—H; 3—BOa; 4, 5—H; 6—CU; 7—BBa; 8—P; 9—H; 10—L; 11—CU; 12—BBa
126: 1, 2—L; 3—H; 4—L; 5, 6—BOa; 7—FB
127: 1—HS; 2—BBb; 3—HS; 4, 5—H; 6—FA; 7, 8—L; 9—FA; 10—R
128: 1—FA; 2—BBa; 3—P; 4—H; 5, 6—P; 7—FA; 8—P
129: 1—M; 2—H; 3—FA; 4—H; 5 through 7—FA
130: 1 through 8—FA
131: 1—BBa; 2—BBb; 3—BBa; 4—H; 5—M; 6—H; 7—BBb; 8—FA; 9 through 11—H
132: 1—BIa; 2 through 4—H; 5 through 7—FA; 8 through 11—H; 12, 13—CU; 14—H
133: 1, 2—P; 3 through 7—H; 8—FA; 9—P
134: 1—H; 2—BBa; 3 through 6—H; 7—BOa

Plate

135: 1, 2—H; 3, 4—FA; 6, 7—H; 8—BOa; 9—L; 10 through 12—H

136: 1 through 9—H; 10—BP; 11—BU; 12—BP

137: 1—BBb; 2—FA; 3—M; 4—H; 5, 6—BOb; 7—BBa; 8—R; 9—M; 10—BBb

138: 1—H; 2—M; 3—BBb; 4—H; 5—FA; 6, 7—M

139: 1—BBb; 2—FA; 3—BBb; 4—M; 5—H; 6, 7—M; 8, 9—BBb

140: 1—BOa; 2—H; 3—BOa; 4, 5—H

141: 1—FA; 2, 3—H; 4—FA; 5—M; 6, 7—H; 8—BIa

142: 1—H; 2—BIb; 3—FA; 4—BOb; 5—FA; 6—H; 7—FA; 8—BIb

143: 1, 2—BBb; 3—H; 4—FA; 5—BBb; 6—H; 7 through 9—BBb

144: 1 through 3—H; 4—R; 5—BBa; 6—FA; 7—H

145: 1—FA; 2—BOb; 3—H; 4—BBb; 5—FA; 6—H; 7—FA; 8—BBb; 9, 10—FA

146: 1, 2—BBb; 3, 4—BBa; 5—BOa; 6—H; 7—BOa; 8—BBa; 9—H

147: 1—FA; 2—BBb; 3, 4—H; 5—FA; 6—H; 7—HS; 8—H; 9—BBa; 10—FA; 11—BBb

148: 1—H; 2—BOa; 3—BBa; 4—H; 5—BBa; 6—FA; 7—BBb; 8—BBa; 9—BP

149: 1—H; 2—Q; 3—FA; 4—D; 5—BBa; 6 through 8—FA; 9 through 11—H; 12—FA; 13—R; 14—BBa; 15, 16—H

150: 1 through 4—H; 5—FA; 6—H; 7—D; 8—BBb; 9—HS; 10—BBa; 11—H

151: 1 through 4—H; 5—R; 6, 7—H

152: 1, 2—H; 3—BOa; 4—H; 5—P; 6—BBa; 7—P; 8—H; 9—P; 10—H

153: 1—P; 2—H; 3 through 5—P; 6—HS; 7—H

154: 1 through 7—H

155: 1—BOa; 2—BBa; 3—FA; 4, 5—H; 6—CU; 7, 8—H; 9—P

156: 1, 2—H; 3—BOa; 4—BBa; 5—BOa; 6—H; 7—BP; 8, 9—H

157: 1—H; 2—FA; 3—H; 4—FA; 5—CU; 6—H; 7—FA; 8—H; 9—R

158: 1—BBb; 2—BBa; 3—P; 4—FA; 5—H; 6—R; 7—H

159: 1, 2—P; 3—H; 4, 5—P

160: 1—H; 2—M; 3—H; 4—M; 5—BBb; 6—H

161: 1—CU; 2, 3—H; 4, 5—FA; 6 through 8—H

162: 1—D; 2, 3—H; 4—P; 5—H; 6—FA; 7—HS; 8—P

163: 1—H; 2—BBa; 3—H; 4—FA; 5—CU; 6—BBa; 7, 8—FA; 9—BBb

164: 1—R; 2—D; 3, 4—BBa; 5, 6—H; 7—BBa; 8—H; 9—BBa; 10—L; 11, 12—BBa

165: 1—BBa; 2—H; 3—BBb; 4—H; 5—BBb; 6—M; 7—BBa

166: 1, 2—BBb; 3—FA; 4—BIb; 5—L; 6—FA; 7—H; 8—BBa

167: 1—BBa; 2—H; 3—BBb; 4—H; 5, 6—FB; 7—BBa; 8—FA; 9—H

168: 1—H; 2—SU; 3—CU; 4—BBb; 5—FB; 6 through 8—H; 9—FA; 10—BBa

169: 1—R; 2—BBa; 3—P; 4 through 7—FA

170: 1—D; 2—M; 3—L; 4—M; 5—BBa; 6—FA; 7, 8—BBa; 9—L

171: 1—BEa; 2—BBb; 3—BOa; 4, 5—FA; 6—BBb; 7—L; 8—BBa; 9—BBb

172: 1—P; 2—BOa; 3 through 5—P; 6—H; 7—FA; 8—BOa; 9—H

Plate

173: 1—H; 2—CU; 3 through 5—P; 6—CU; 7, 8—H

174: 1 through 8—P

175: 1 through 7—P; 8—FA

176: 1—M; 2, 3—H; 4—BOa; 5—P; 6, 7—H; 8—BBa; 9—BBb

177: 1, 2—P; 3 through 5—FA

178: 1 through 12—H

179: 1 through 3—H; 4—CR; 5—H; 6—CR; 7—H; 8—CR; 9—H

180: 1 through 5—H; 6, 7—CR; 8 through 11—H

181: 1 through 12—H

182: 1, 2—P; 3—CU; 4—H

183: 1 through 12—H

184: 1, 2—R; 3 through 10—H

185: 1 through 9—H

186: 1 through 12—H

187: 1—M; 2—H; 3—BBb; 4—R; 5 through 7—H

188: 1—P; 2—BBb; 3—P; 4 through 8—H; 9—BBa; 10—BBb; 11—H

189: 1—FA; 2 through 9—H

190: 1 through 4—H; 5—BOb; 6, 7—H; 8—BBb; 9 through 12—H

191: 1 through 3—H; 4—FA; 5—BBb; 6, 7—FA; 8—H

192: 1—FA; 2—CU; 3—H; 4—BOb; 5—CU; 6, 7—H; 8—R

193: 1—M; 2 through 4—BBb; 5—H; 6—BBb

194: 1—FA; 2 through 4—H; 5—P; 6—BBb

195: 1—H; 2—CU; 3, 4—H; 5—HS; 6 through 8—H; 9—CU; 10—H

196: 1—FA; 2—H; 3—FA; 4—BOb; 5—FA; 6—BBa; 7, 8—H

197: 1 through 3: H; 4, 5—CU; 6—H; 7—HS; 8, 9—CU; 10 through 12—H

198: 1—P; 2—H; 3—FA; 4—H

199: 1—D; 2—H; 3—R; 4—CU; 5—H

200: 1, 2—H; 3—FA; 4—H; 5, 6—FA; 7, 8—H

201: 1 through 3—H; 4—CU; 5 through 7—H

202: 1, 2—H; 3—BBa; 4—FA; 5, 6—BBa; 7—H

203: 1 through 6—H

204: 1 through 3—H; 4—FA; 5—H; 6—FA; 7—R

205: 1 through 3—FA; 4, 5—H; 6—BP; 7—FA; 8—H

206: 1 through 9—H

207: 1 through 7—R; 8—H; 9 through 12—R

208: 1 through 5—H

209: 1 through 4—H

210: 1 through 3—H; 4—SP

211: 1, 2—H; 3—CU; 4 through 7—BOa; 8—CU; 9, 10—BOa; 11 through 13—CU; 14—H

212: 1 through 7—FA

213: 1 through 7—FA

214: 1 through 7—FA

215: 1, 2—H; 3—FA; 4, 5—H; 6, 7—FA; 8, 9—H; 10—FA

216: 1, 2—FA; 3, 4—M; 5—H; 6—FA

217: 1, 2,—H; 3—FA; 4 through 6—H; 7, 8—BBa; 9—BOa; 10—D; 11—H; 12—BBa; 13, 14—H

218: 1, 2—P; 3—FA; 4—R; 5, 6—H

219: 1, 2—H; 3—BOa; 4 through 8—H; 9, 10—BOa

220: 1—H; 2—BOa; 3 through 5—H

Plate

221: 1 through 5—H
222: 1 through 4—H
223: 1—H; 2—FA; 3—HS; 4—H; 5—BP; 6—HS; 7—H; 8—BBa
224: 1—L; 2, 3—H; 4—BP; 5—H; 6—BP; 7—H; 8, 9—FA; 10—H; 11—R; 12, 13—BBa; 14, 15—H; 16—BP

Plate

225: 1 through 8—H
226: 1 through 4—H; 5—BOa; 6, 7—H; 8—BBa; 9 through 14—H
227: 1 through 14—H
228: 1 through 14—H
229: 1 through 12—H

INDEX OF ILLUSTRATIONS